AS LORDS EXPECTED

Roy Blackman

AS LORDS EXPECTED

Liz

with all good wishes

Roy.

Rockingham Press

Published by
The Rockingham Press
11 Musley Lane,
Ware, Herts
SG12 7EN

British Library Cataloguing-in-Publication Data

A catalogue record for this book
is available from the British Library

ISBN 1 873468 44 X

Printed in Great Britain
by Bemrose Shafron (Printers) Ltd,
Chester

Printed on Recycled Paper

What matters is not the achievement,
but the struggle.

For Michael Laskey
— the better manufactor,
and the Arvon Foundation
— the manufactory.

Acknowledgements

My thanks to the editors of the following publications, in which some of these poems first appeared:

Envoi, Foolscap, The Frogmore Papers, Grand Piano, The Honest Ulsterman, Lines Review, Margin, Other Poetry, Outposts, Pennine Platform, Poetry Nottingham, The Rialto, Seam, Slow Dancer, South West Poetry Competition Anthology, Spokes, Stand, Staple and *Thames Poetry.*

Some of the poems were written, and many heavily revised, while a Hawthornden Fellow in 1993.

Contents

Donkey

It was wartime. She was only doing her duty,
that Ward Sister,
who wouldn't let you in to see me
once, when I broke my leg at twenty months.
There were rules.
She couldn't have unsettling mothers
wrinkling the covers on her beds.
Instead, you made me a little grey
stuffed felt donkey with harness and saddle,
a girth strap round his fat middle,
a tail and mane in nugget-brown
flat, slightly irregular cut strips
whose free ends were more rigid
than the bends hugged tightly to his neck.
Four firm legs, of comforting turgor,
sprang back when forced apart; he sat
on the rail at the foot of my bed
until they took him away.
There were rules.
He never came back.
The leg healed.

Above it all

At the top of my ringing flight things look
quite different: above both roundabouts and swings.
The evening light is yellow, thick and weak.
The last of my last day. Tomorrow: school.
Mummy is small and very far away,
wearing her worried 'I'm sorry' smile.
We never even liked playing hide-and-seek.

Clutching the upright piping either side
I crouch, then sit on the sounding iron grating.
My crêpe-heeled sandals judder, squeal and cling,
inching out my bare calves on the curving brass.

Across the rift of years, the did-not-dares,
all their contempt; all yours; his sneers;
how can I back down now, to run to you,
edge past that clambering, jammed,
righteous, spiteful queue? The ground begins
to spin, tilt, turn away. Mother, I will come!
Each night I practise - hard - that letting go.

Of Andrew Riley

Reading the paper makes me stand
behind Sandra Riley while she drowned her son.

He shouted out: "Don't kill me, Mum"
and she held him down.

"Don't kill me, Mum". He knew what she would do.
He'd seen her missing from her face before.

"He struggled and almost climbed out twice"
she told them. But she held him down.

I need the reports of her blank stare in the court,
her previous history.
I need to believe his eyes are turned away from me,
to see him panic.

She destroyed a demon,
removed some vermin,
not her Andrew.

And he fought not his loved, imperfect mother,
not even as a person overpowered,
but just as a dumb animal: for life.

"Don't kill me, Mum"

Growing Pains

Three years forever mother's loved one,
now the new baby lords it, in his pram!
"I can't walk. My legs hurt. Push me."
"Oh no you don't — poor old man!
You mustn't moan about your brother:
he can't walk; you can."
"I can't. My legs keep hurting. Push
me up the hill. I won't walk any more!"
"Oh yes you will."

Then waking in the night, still moaning;
crying when got out of bed.
A real pain; always grizzling. Was it
more than sulking, a bear's sore head?
The family doctor plainly puzzled.
"Growing pains" kind neighbours said.
"I've had the test results; he can't be ill."
"He isn't growing out of it."
"No — but he will."

Till one night: fever, thin limbs rigid;
a rash, but features pale and strained.
Rushed to Great Ormond Street; each hump
in the everlasting country lanes
hurt. An epidural — cracking apart
each back-bone, bruising their knuckled pain.
"Die now, my son." Not meningitis:
"Still's Disease. He'll never walk again."
"Oh yes he will."

Near to tears, forcing him through
each exercise, each grinding morning drill.

Knew she was hurting him, knew she would have to,
whatever doctors and neighbours might say.
Near to tears on his first Sports Day:
last, but running.

Shame

Our first opera; my mother's too,
here on a visit to us nearly newly-marrieds.
Fidelio on tour: how ludicrous
the wrinkled yellow latex skullcaps
of shaven prisoners; how gut-clutching
their shuffling hymn to sunlight.
In the interval, eating overpriced ice-creams,
I introduce her to some new, well-dressed friends
from Jill's Medical Physics Department.

She had to leave school at fifteen
even though she'd won a place for teacher-training.
Her Dad, who was more than rich enough,
refused to pay. Seduced, pregnant, married
young, five kids, a long lifetime's
uncertain low wages later, she's nervous, jerky,
drops some ice-cream, tries to rub it
into the carpet with her shoe. I keep
talking. Nobody says anything.
We go back to Florestan's black dungeon.

Afterwards, she says how beautiful
Beethoven is; she didn't know.

The Cornflake Packet

With Dad as good as gone, Mum got no money.
Club for a while, and a bit prised from the State,
but Mum, once a London sawmill-owner's daughter,
now had to go out char-ing.

When I got in, lugging a bag of homework,
I turned the light on, drew the curtains, set
the table, laid and lit the open fire,
took off my scarf and coat.

Canvassed in the cloisters at Sir William Borlase's School,
I didn't refuse free dinners and travel passes
or being given Scripture Union schools-camp
holidays in Devon.

She turned cuffs and collars, let down trousers,
let out seams; never allowed herself
to feel unwell.

I grew greens and spuds on Dad's allotment
— Arran Pilot, Maris Piper, Pentland Dell —
manhandled logs for firewood on my bike,
worked endless Saturday mornings at the chemists,
stocking shelves for kind, cross Mr. Soar.

We ate mince, fried with batter;
three of marge to one of butter.
I had no means of feeling insecure;
never council-housed, or shabby:
worn grey cardboard-suitcase poor.

Only now do the colours come back vivid:
the yellow, green, red, white of the cornflake packet
she cut into insoles to cover the hole in her shoe.

Pippin Returned

Warm, the tongue between the worn, clenched teeth
but the limbs relaxed, tail curved up over her flank,
the lower forepaw spread out as a cushion for her jaw,
the way she slept, for fifteen banked-up summers,
                                        in the sun;
but the head tipped back now, one half-open eye
already blueing after the vein's injection,
our last due the only true immunity from pain.
I lift her carefully (why?) out of the carrying-box
while Jill is indoors and the children still at school,
set her down gently, ease the tongue back in,
but, shutting the mouth, I have to feel again
the soft throat, jaw-ridge, bristly chin she most loved
me to rub, stretching up, eyes closed, and grinning.

But rearrange her neatly, each precision pad
which pricked its way between the washing-up
tucked in, and wrap the vibrant patchwork —
tortoiseshell blacks and tans, tabby-patterned gingers,
whitenesses of fur, that gave such purring pleasure
to fondle — tight in a piece of old white sheet.
Put the floppy bundle in a new black plastic dustbin bag
and lay all in an empty freezer basket till her burial
below that largest rockery sarsen stone I shall engrave.
I leave the emptied box with lid thrown back
                                        in case they see it
and wonder, and dismayed, are too afraid to look.

Last year my eldest sister had to stick it out;
at eighty-six, it's probably my mother next;
but how could I quiet her last distress?

Sure and Certain

I

The privilege of kneeling at her swollen feet
to ease on slippers passes soon
as fewer, briefer walkings drift into waking dreams,
the walls, floor, corners, ceiling of the room
becoming so much farther, dimmer than they seem.
Now it is my turn to guide the spoon,
tip it, scrape the food against the upper lip,
control the baby's cup and gently break
a lifetime's grip on the handle.

II

I tentatively bathe both velcro'd eyelids,
firmly brush the peeling tongue,
insert one pill below it, push
the other up against the upper gum,
remembering Melinda's teething;
empty the catheter bag, spray Yardley's Lavender,
help on the assault course to the commode:
poor, sore, wrinkled flesh
that sons should never see.
These are legendary times: the bedroom air
heavy with a focused life, each wandering gesture,
Delphic phrase, discussed by Gwen.
I'm happy just to watch
the blank stare weakly turn and smile;
to hold her hand.

III

Stopping her falling out of bed again,
off to catch her coach to Scotland,

16

I sit on the edge, my strong right arm
trembling to support her hot, bowed back
as her head sinks slowly sideways to my shoulder.
'I'm such an old misery' she sighs 'to you and Doff'.
I say not so; I say how brave;
how proud...   our love...

And then she must be firmly tucked back in
and I must be off to catch my train
now Don is here.
I bend to kiss my Mum; 'I'll be back soon'.
Did she say that, when she left
me in the hospital at twenty months?

Being left. Having to leave.
Such an old misery.

IV

The area mortician, young and plump,
staying late for us
(has he a date tonight?)
because Don's train's delayed again,
gently hurries us in.

Stiffened as though
for a faced-down blow,
so little, old, and cere,
and oh, so cold.
In turn, I cry:
that I should come to this.

V

Grouped around Dad's grave,
the ministers, in blowing robes, conclude

fond prayers, proffer their sure and certain hopes.
Discreetly passed the dust in a dice-cup,
held, dazed and observant, by Melinda's hand,
I duly obliterate the name, machine-engraved
on a skimped brass strip, leaving only the dates:
nineteen oh one to ninety one.

Dorothy Sophia Blackman's dead.
She is my mother now.

Working at the World

I walk, in the strengthening sun's compassionate leave,
to the shops;
smell privet, roses, the Co-op baking bread;
work at the world
as a full and vivid place.

They are so gone from us, the dead;
so not-there in our world.
I feel — uncoupled from my life;
not alone; but surrounded
by a great space.

The list insensibly ticked-off,
I walk back, carrying the racking bags
of groceries.
For meals, presumably.
How one dead can crowd out all the living.

Springs eternal

Clots of may, clinging where flung;
a hare's ears semaphore across spring wheat;
white-throats nesting in vivid new ivy;
hedge-parsley atomised from surging banks;

but every two months it comes, in green and white,
this catalogue of torture, 'disappearance';
false imprisonment, and rape;
and I must fight off the comfort of despair,
write to Your Excellency, Belgrave Square
and imposing Palaces of Justice, elsewhere;
waste time and heart and money
for one small slug of righteousness,
for good not yet quite threadbare.

Each Christmas, on cards of evergreen and snow,
to sun-struck, sand-blasted wastes of prison-yards,
we write: 'Keep up your hope'.

Ponary

*"In the fourth pit they found 24,000 corpses, which
included [among the Jews] many Soviet prisoners of
war, a number of Poles, Catholic priests and nuns,
and one German soldier."*

Reuben Ainsztein: *Jewish Resistance in Nazi-
occupied Eastern Europe* (Paul Elek, London)

Shot for hoarding gold
torn from exterminated vermin
which rightly belonged to the Reich.
That seems most likely.
If not a blackmailer silenced.
Or the result of a lover's quarrel
over a pretty Polish prostitute.

Maybe a settling of old scores
between a card-cheat and his debtor.
A deserter, perhaps, afraid
of being posted to the Eastern Front.
Possibly one who, exasperated,
at last hit back
at a particularly brutal NCO.

Dare we hope enough
to think he may have been a patriot
stumbling, trying to keep his balance
in the crumbling sand, who, on the brink,
had to believe the seething evidence
and made his totally useless gesture:
he protested?

Als ich kan

Educated eyes will recognise
those patches of close cross-hatching
as darkness. It was night.

Enlightened minds will find
these parallel lines of ink
to be the piles of straw
torn from that mattress
on a floor left mainly blank.
They were asleep.

So deep, innate our grace,
we understand the feelings on a face
composed of nothing but the strokes
of burins in a master's hand.
These curves show two men's eyes,
like O's. Their mouths are opened
wide. They are afraid.

Arrays of sigmoids form the braid
of cords by which their wrists are tied
to hooks set high in the wall
above each head. They cannot move.

All this skill to prove
that we know what it is to love,
be fully human; how to touch.

Laughing at us over his shoulder,
the foreground shows a Renaissance soldier
with a torch.

Two Observations near Rosewell, Midlothian

In the old days this farm would have had a horse-drawn gin.
The horse would have worked its circle for hour after hour,
turning the horizontal wheel to power
threshers, winnowers, dockers, shearers, churns.
Now it's a stud farm. The horse is still tied to a gin,
a thing like a flimsy overgrown playground roundabout,
but power is fed to a central motor to spin
it slowly, walking the racehorse as it turns.

Nearby, two men, in an open-cast coalmine, with brooms.
When the last ochre layer is scraped off and dumped
                                        in the tipper
they brush the black underlay clean for the waiting ripper.
A village of miners reduced to two road-sweepers; grooms.

The voluntary Red Cross stroke-patient rehabilitation scheme

Jim has had a stork

Jim can not read or ride

bits of his mind have ˙hide

he car not find them

if I say "find the letter b"

then he can do it

if I say "what is that?"

he does note know it is a 'b'

Jim calls a big white bird with a long neck

and wide web feet   "a swa - llow?"

Jim gets sad he can not read

Jim gets so mad he can not read 'se - ah - de'

he did red such a lot — his eye
skimming the pages with an unfelt airy grace,
the mind's unthinking rare dexterity, recognising,
swooping, snapping up the black motes as they danced
in sequence down the lines of flight
as your eye has just done,

as Ministers' and Treasury officials' must do
every day they audit cash-flows, settle
their accounts with the National Health Service,
that proud white bird of power in achievement, serving all,
which had no need to trumpet, bugle-call its fame,
the very wing-beats of its drive and purpose
                                        made the mute air sing
and now is dying of incompetence or militant neglect,
to all our shame. An untrained, part-time volunteer

can not help Jim

for him and all the poor

the book is on the other foot

Heirlooms

I wear your watch, last of the family valuables unhocked,
but missing its thick gold chain with all the fobs:
the bloodstone I believed must hold real blood;
the black intaglio head with spikes all round
— like Liberty's — that swivelled in a gold horseshoe;
a carved red seal (carnelian?) whose imprint
I don't remember seeing; a clear moss-agate, I think —
all gone, like the tools we had to sell. Your 'stoosh'
                                   cleared out,
though we never found the money that Mum thought
you must have hidden somewhere down The Shed.
Your stippling brushes: bristles in posh cardboard boxes,
embossed straw-varnished handles poking through.
The wide sign-writer's palette (I never understood
the wooden maul, just like a big bass-drum stick).
I wanted to put my favourite items by
while trying to price the others (far too high!)
from your latest Miller, Morris & Brooker booklet.
We had to take what we could get. The palette went.
But I still have the best — heraldically yours:
the cut-down putty-trowel with our 'B' in rubbed
                                   brass brads;
the broad horn-handled pocket-knife, worn-down
                                   in the trenches;
and the watch, gold case engraved with your initials.
As for the rest — I have inherited:
I studied geology; still enjoy calligraphy.

A Work-Ethic

I swing on the green wooden gate by the sweet-spiked
                                                    lavender;
I sing my incantation to the gravel road:
— Da — dee — Da — dee — Da — so he will come
wheeling the orange-cream steps on his upright bike,
the handlebars a yoke for his pot of brushes,
paint-tins forced at an angle on their thin wire arcs,
turps in a can with its screw-cap tea-pot spout
slung by a knotted loop of clothes-line clogged
with paints, but rubbed spots show its chevron weave.
He'll smile to see me, leave his work against the hedge,
stoop to hug and kiss me, lift me up
on his shoulders to show me the moss and feather cup
in the lilac fork, holding — so tightly, so gently —
three chaffinch eggs, whose thinnest dribbles of dark
                                                    brown paint
bear their indecipherable message: I love you, son.
I will not look up, to find, when he has gone by,
the ragged nest, whose floor lets in the empty sky,
or the one egg, impaled on a dead, yolk-lacquered twig.

Painter and Decorator

My father did his best. His one day of rest
was roast meat and potatoes after beer
and cribbage in The Crispin with his friends;
an after-dinner doze. Perhaps, in Sunday Best,
we'd walk The Cutting, out across The Fields
to Taplow, and then back past Hitcham Church
and The Gore which, he said, was a battlefield.

No day-dreamer, as the eldest boy he had to help
his abandoned mother take in village laundry
(something about a gamekeeper being shot).
Grandfather finally came back, sick and broke
from making his fortune in Africa, to die.
(Or so the family always thought;
turns out he'd really been in Reading Gaol.)

Apprenticed into steam, my Dad returned
from Wipers and the Somme shrapnelled and gassed.
He was pre-war — some enterprising chap
had driven through traction engines in a tank.
He retrained with a decorating firm
through the turnip twenties, set up on his own,
and brought the five of us up by his craft.

He could scumble, stipple, mottle, stain and grain,
but after World War Two there was no call for it.
He sold the barrow with his own sign-writing
                                        on the sides;
wheeled ladders, cans and brushes on his bike.
We stopped sending overalls and linen to the laundry.
He would not work for others, skimp or cheat,
or give up, go down the Trading Estate for a wage.

He kept up for a good while but, weak-chested now,
lost out in winter; worked and worried hard to make
a steadily smaller living. I've read his ledger, seen
the wobbly left-hand writing from the first stroke.
Three hundred pounds he made in his last year.
He never got his pension from the War Office:
'his illnesses were not a direct result'.

The Candle

Long after he was gone, the candle stayed;
smudges in its perfect microcrystalline wax bowl,
black flecks in arrested tears hung frozen from its rim.

After supper, Dad went down The Shed
to stand, blending and straining paints
through doubled stockings stretched across a can.
The candle stood between three angled nails
tacked in a quadrilateral scrap of wood
pinned, like a bracket, to the window-frame.
I sometimes used to watch, until bedtime,
softly-lit mysteries and troubled shadows.

I had a stand-up bike when I was seven —
second or seventh hand, I wouldn't know —
he wanted to paint it, make it look more new;
not electric blue, not racy red,
but a kind of coach-work translucent maroon
perhaps he'd seen as posh on some client's car.
I think he wanted me to want that colour
I want to think the best that he could do.

I light its black wick, let the hot tears flow,
grip it, scald my hand and mind, and with the flame
burn out the blackness — let my father go.

Frozen Prawns

Are we always who we were?
Mayflies trapped in gum?
Just emerged, I watched my Mum
struggling with my struck-dumb Dad.
A strong man in a cot — or half a man:
on one side hung cold meat.

He couldn't speak or read or write his name.
Visits dragged unmiracled, like his foot.
We smuggled in beer to cheer him, tried to chat.
I never thought of dominoes or cards:
he taught me crib; a treat on Sunday night.
He might have liked still beating me at that.

Sometimes he'd grip me with his left hand — hard —
and shake me, growling; hate under thick eyebrows.
Then his wet stubble would rasp my unshaved cheek.
I grew up: like bindweed in a pipe.
Sometimes he'd make his right arm shake, and wail —
not sob — and work his leg to judder and jerk.

We had him home a few times, for the day.
Getting him to the lav, taking his trousers down,
helping to wipe him off, wasn't child's play
but when the ambulance came back! They had
to come to numb the other half, to get him
out of the house and driven away.

So we went there on Sundays
and took him, what with bus fares,
Mum thought to be the best that we could do:
adding to his thin-sliced piece of bread and marge
the sweet and salty taste of peeled and frozen prawns.
Tender flesh for his soft gums to chew.

An Outing for the Quieter Ones

Here we all are, in the huge auditorium, hushed
to hear how the great creator patterns
our monotone or noisy world.
Silent,
we listen
as powerful fingers
chop and partition the air.
Notes bell, abut, trill, intercut, concatenate;
shelling the unseen still Botticellian ear,
afloat in a tress-strewn and breeze-borne, a rose-blown
mandala of sea-sound alone;
the whole round me
alone
until applause pops back the audience.

We puzzle that the pianist must be helped down
                                    the platform steps
but then distorted pieces interlock:
the blind performer can see better
the music the deaf composer writes,
hearing the signal from white-noise,
seeing the patterns in the snow.
Should we have let
Captain Oates go?

The Doctor's Story

The depressed ones often come to me and say:
'Its all so pointless'.
I desperately want to cheer them on:
'Well done. Hooray. You've got it!
There is no point to anything we do,
to us, the world, the Universe, morning dew,
it just is; we just are; and that's the point.
We don't have to do anything;
we don't have to be anyone.
You're depressed — oh yes, well that's brain-chemistry,
but also probably because you're trying to be
somebody you're not: a person with a point.
You feel you should be one God would appoint:
good and true, successful, happy, well, while you
are not. Don't feel like that.
We aren't put on this earth
to suffer or work out.
We aren't put on this earth.
Don't look for a purpose or a plan
to justify your pain: it isn't punishment.
There is no Plan we can advance,
no Purpose our defeat can hinder.
The whole world's futile just as much as purposive;
it doesn't matter if you 'win' or 'fail':
happiness is allowed.'
But if I did, they'd go away and overdose.
I just hand out the pills they want and say: 'You'll see.
It *will* get better; I can guarantee.'
And take a few myself to keep them company.

Traumerei

For many years, when I was young,
I had the one recurrent dream:
running, running after that platform,
arm stretched out for its thick black column,
straining as hard as I possibly could, but
just missing the double-decker bus
and the whole street jeering.

Psychiatrists have come and gone;
we've worked so hard at who I am
I've changed my dream:
I'm in the warm red bus at last
safely watching the street go past
at a hell of a lick, and look:
there's no one in the driving seat.

A Chichester Monument

Seven hundred years of self-effacement:
the Purbeck Marble slowly exfoliating,
rubbling its drifts of knubbly snail shells
two hundred thousand times as dead.
I need the guide-book entry for the Retro-Quire:
"On the north wall, a much worn memorial to Maude,
Countess of Warenne and Surrey (died twelve thirty six)".

Above the level grey-green waste protrude
two wrists: rounded, finished, polished.
Their attitude is that of prayer,
directing where her defaced head should be,
but these two planed-off hands don't meet:
they hold some object, chalice-shaped but stemless.
The wrists form inclined mid-ribs to a recessed
trefoil panel; the gracefully curved hands
and precious burden form the third.

I see. There never was an effigy to bear
a stylised likeness of her breathless face
forever to new worshippers.
What astounding certitude of worth
allowed the Countess Maude
humility to scorn her birth,
the blazons, robes, her lauded face
for a plain slab lid,
confident that the Trinity
would cherish and uplift her inner being,
seeing only what the guide-book states:
"the hands holding the heart".

As Lords Expected

"Everyone" my friend Don Smith
the new psychiatrist said, "is born
Perfect, Immortal and Omnipotent.
Only slowly do we learn."
Most, it seems, are happily fobbed-off
with love, care, courage of whoever parents them.
But some are cheated of their birthright,
early come to NO they are not lovely
in themselves, are no more worthy
— worse, were never worthy; blind
to every proof of love another bares to them,
are not deceived; cannot believe.

Successful forty years in spheres
they've chosen to surround them,
they peer through agitated snow
from the castellations of their topmost keeps
at storehouses, banqueting-halls,
warm withdrawing rooms, bed-chambers,
morning-rooms, galleries, formal gardens, and beyond:
their lands; cool woods, ripe corn, bright vines,
green pastures, farms and workshops, fair markets,
colleges of debate, far lodges, and beyond:
the constellations of their friends' estates.

With all that country round at peace
they don't know how to fight
their own way out to "enter unannounced
as lords that are certainly expected and yet
there is a silent joy at their arrival".

*(The quotation is from S.T. Coleridge's own gloss on
stanza 10 of Part IV of 'The Rime of the Ancient Mariner')*

Melinda's Gift

"And Daddy, for Christmas, if you're not too busy,
only if you can spare the time, I mean,
I would like a little baby cradle for my dolls' house.
I haven't got a cradle. Please."

I felt obliged to try:
the plywood too thick and easily splintered,
but covered up with two coats of 'brilliant white gloss'
it mightn't look so bad.

It looked so mean.
I got out paints and tapered brushes
to tart it up a bit with flowers
in red and yellow and green.

Let's see: dry bristle-work for frizzed carnations.
That looks quite good. A full brush for foliage
and a sure-stroked snail surge wakes a leaf flute
green across a frozen sea!

Be generous then; risk drips for tipped-in pimpernels
whose lopsided petallings
turn to a rich perspective;
and on this side a single loaded hair,

dragged and twisted, coils a tendril,
catches hold and riots up my outlook.
Not such intense delight in many weeks
as in this worked-at present.

Thank you, Melinda.

There and Back Again

He is, I think, four.
He's up The Trenches where
picnics and wild strawberries are.
He's lying a little apart
in a place by himself — his fort —
in sunshine through his shirt
like snuggling on the spot where Mummy's
hot-water bottle has just been.
His cheek's pressed on a scratchy nest of grass.
He looks through a stockade of stalks
and rough leaves covered with a lace
of broken rainbows, dancing when he moves.
His right eye sees a beetle with a long thin nose,
grey, but just as dusted red-green fuzzy.
He's walking up a leaf of grass.
His legs work very quickly.
He's patting at his footpath
with feelers like two fingers
as he slowly nods his whole head up and down
and sudden, I feel afresh that flash he feels
my first discovered day:
'I am me — looking at the beetle'.

And then he is thirty-seven,
sat on the bedside by the folded linen,
frightened of the sunshine outside on the garden,
and turned to the unstoppably stepping down
print of the patterned wall.
Through repetitious gush of pointless tears
that promise is clamped tight about his forehead,
a Nodding Donkey pumps it up and down:
'There's nowhere else to go; no one to turn to.
You are you and only you can cure it'.

Slowly, feebly, feeling his own way
back up the buckled road from which he's fallen,
shyly standing, one hand on the doorway to his adit,
blinking in so late a morning light,
rainbow-glossed, sun-blizzarded, kin-welcomed.
Not too late to sit and eat
wild strawberries at the picnic;
that vital taste of honeycomb;
those hot white flakes of fish.

The Robin

and when I let my Black Monk tempt to misery,
run from the perfection I have set for me,
and sit to weep my weak-kneed inability to cope,
the robin, on impossibly thin limbs, comes, trampolining.

Rest Harrow

Valerian on the cliffs and five white doves
circle in bright but unsunned air
and come to rest.
Here, on the testing edge,
water is dictated to by water which allows
itself to be dictated to by water.
Weed follows. A frond of Fucus, waving.

Calmly, the light comes on,
wrinkling the liquid skin.
In the unfrozen bowl, a pool of clear lime,
wavelets lollop pebbles into praise of time's long grinding.
A bell-note. Lithic tympani. Glissando.

Come away. Contemplation is an art
for those without dependants.
Back to the hog hotel, the business-conference breakfast.
Become a weed again among the world-consuming
                                    worlds of men.

Samphire makes the most of stone's grey hospitality,
celebrating pocks and cracks in rock's stern face,
incensed by her sweetly fennel scent
from pieces passers-by have tossed away.

I greet a celadon-jade snail, bearing a bronze and
                                    old-gold shell
over a cigarette butt. Even disease in the leaves of
                                    this sycamore tree
shines with the fretted depth and intricacy
of Chinese carved red lacquer.

Cammock, a delicate tea-cup pink and white,
ornaments tough spiny stems from obstinate
                                        wire-cored roots;
enough, in the slogging horse-drawn days,
to bring an abrupt halt to harrowing,

and here, at the end of a Corporation hand-rail,
"No person shall climb above this beach.
                                Penalty Fifty Pounds",
a hero has taken his standard length of iron pipe
and worked it to a party-blower, a galvanised curlicue.

Each time

I come, all but
the core of it
has changed a little more:
a tree down here,
a new wire fence,
the weir repaired,
that top leat cleared,
mill-pond reclaimed,
path ditched and drained,
a gate, a hand-rail
and a stile
to reach the patched
stone churchyard wall.
This year, another
small depression:
her coffin has
at last caved in.

There Again

You may try to fight, to clarify,
but unattended thoughts thicken the sky,
signs of silent visitation multiply.

My sunlit Crystal Palace dims
and glazes to a cramped cheap greenhouse
which, like the bike and lack of boat,
provokes the road's polite contempt.
The flaring Scarlet Pimpernel becomes a creeping weed.

Visored with stupor, I stare at the floor,
sack arms dragging at slackened shoulders;
shuffle lead boots through dirt and trash.

What survives is never love —
that they can take away —
but stroking a cat, eating when hungry,
mugs of sweet tea, defaecation,
hot baths, a warm bed: these pleasures stay.

I wait for sun on green uncurling fronds;
for that huge underminer of each universe:
the cyclical brain-chemistry of hope.

This Morning

at last I thought it might be worth my getting up:
the cistern played me 'Raindrops on a Pond'.

Now quartz grains round out light
from crumbled compost.

Under stirred ashes, matt black starts to spark
and spread a low blue fume.

I see where a wasp has begun to chew
through the old oak gate-post.

I will write clouds like cauliflowers
ballooning by.

Blood Doning

Absent sixteen years on drugs:
a quiet celebration.
Ritual prick of the proffered finger,
capillary rise of fraternal red,
a litany of health, forswearing AIDS;
found worthy of the crumbs under the table,
the password of my name, age and address
ushers me through each screen of initiation
to reach the ranks of couches for this love-feast,
jacket neatly folded across my shanks.
Cuff inflated, the unseen needle
painlessly inserted in my vein,
I grasp my piece of dowel and calmly pump
while meditating on a row of nails
in the fibreboard ceiling.
For once a patient giving, not receiving,
my starving heart is tapped at need and will.
Return to citizenship:
at six-month intervals to feel,
at least for an hour, part of the nation;
this mystic communion of its briefly true elite,
sharing tea and biscuits
at the bar of the Carnival Hall.

Fairy Tale

(after the film 'Ryan's Daughter')

On the evening of her wedding
— that wonder of seven parishes —
flushed above the froth of their lives' worth
of Brussels lace, she descends
the staircase to the Great Hall
where all the males of her village
wait to claim their brute due of a kiss.
Brightening, the idiot presents himself
last of all; abrupt, she sweeps him away
on her disgust, for the girls to ring
and taunt him in their dance.

But when, flaming in the pride of her shame,
she stands waiting for the waggoner
to take her away, and he sees her
— shorn, whipped, her shift torn,
her famous face bruised and puffy —
then mutely signs the register
of his pity and distress:
she sees him, stinking, clumping slobberer,
and tenderly kisses him goodbye.

Choir Practice

One summer evening, after choir, Don
and the bass Bill Walker
(I liked him; sometimes he motor-biked me home.
The wind, speed, freedom; how we slowed, hung, swayed
and flung round corners!) were talking
of Peter Welch, the tenor's, engagement
to Margaret, the fishmonger's daughter
(a pastel-dressed, shyly-smiling woman,
not 'common' as my mother put it,
not like that Rita round the corner:
all high heels, tight skirts and sweaters,
bright lipstick, big earrings, hair-dye)
and I said, surprised: "She isn't very pretty."
Their laugh, my brother's embarrassed:
"That isn't all that counts, you know"
curled me inside my youth and foolishness.

The first time I could do the post at Christmas,
I delivered to new council houses round Lent Green.
I looked through the kitchen window at their happiness.
She recognised me, smiled, gave me a tip.

She walks in beauty

My sister Doff is much too short;
both her friends were much too tall.
Patsy, practical and pretty,
solved the matter,
walking in the gutter when with Doff.
Jane gassed herself.

46

The Bristol Seychelles Expedition
Nineteen Sixty Four to Five

Once, on Aldabra,
I shot a white-eye.
A neat bespectacled bird
the Creoles call 'oiseau lunettes'.
Just one; strictly for scientific purposes.
Such power behind a gun;
the prompt of opportunity:
'Outdo the others — shoot ahead'.
I fired.

After the shock to thorn-scrubbed, sun-bleached rock,
the slow disintegration of the smoke,
I breathed out my relief.
I'd missed:
the bird perched on its twig just as before.

An ornithologist would have retained
his knowledge of passeriforms:
how they can sleep because their body's weight
locks their thin feet, by tendon-threaded legs,
on to the branch. Even an uninformed observer
might have wondered why it didn't fly away.

She slowly bowed towards me
swung
until she hung head down
and dropped.
Warm in my palm,
apparently unharmed
but for two tiny bright red beads
on her white breast,
her light head
flopped
over my clever finger.

Of Infinite Regret

*'A man will have to give account on Judgement Day
of every good thing he could have enjoyed — and didn' t'*
Talmud

Robin sated and asleep, your milk still ran
and you, proud and excited by the suckling,
looked up smiling and invited: "Want some?"

Worried, jealous, self-destructive, I
turned away for ever that unique taste
of shared happiness, those breasts,
never heavier, more generously extended,
and, lips pressed firmly onto emptiness,
tongued the dereliction of a prude:
"No thank you".

A decade later,
looking at your withering dugs
with straighter love, I'm left
this literary consolation prize:
a chance to use the Muse-word — 'bathukolpian'.

Robin's Panther

'Dad I've made Dad Dad I've DAD!
I've made a black panther at school out of pottery
Mrs. Smith told me it looked very good.'
Of course, I thought, I'll have to make the same allowances:
after all, the boy is only six.
He'll have rolled a thick cylinder under his palm
(I remembered the jerk of its cam when it flattened,
the slap as the free end got flailing away).
He'll have stuck on the four paws of pinches of clay,
the tail will be broken (they're always made too thin)
the maw will be massive — (dentition impressive!) —
it'll rock and look daft but that's not what I'll say.
But this
crouches;
it threatens,
head heavy with menace,
the tail in mid-lash as it lines up its prey.
But how? He's no genius; he's not a sculptor —
obstinately ordinary's more the phrase I'd use!
No preconceptions or thought of conventions,
no having-been-taught-how to get in the way.
Just him and the clay, his fingers and notions
working together in what we call play.

Gibson's Mill

Came off plashy January tops
where grass and water shuddered before the wind,
down grit scarps through dripping beauty-spots,
head-down, an intense student of my footing,
toes-first, looking for clog-grooved rocks,
the cotton-workers' paved walkways and steps,
safe where quartzite knuckles whitened through
squeegee humus, masticated leaves and algal slime
that would slip me backlong.

And so I came to Gibson's Mill
where ten-year-olds picked cotton waste.
Weirs faulting the easy shallows
fed into straight and narrow leats,
were hoarded in a black pit high above a bare embankment
and let out in summer droughts through sluices:
sliced, wrapped water set to work a water-wheel,
forced to duck below a road's stone rainbow
past two squat privies at the river's edge
like some developing Third World slum.

Sun mushroomed up through cloud,
enlightened beeches slenderly declared for glory,
an enthroned dipper bobbed to royalty
above a plaque, set in a stone:
    Sing to God
    Sing praises to his name
    Lift up a song to him
    Who rides upon the clouds:
    His name is the Lord
    Exult before him.

Upstream, resistance had provoked a gorge.
I saw
quilts,
sheet-wrinkles,
sleeves gathered to cuff slabs,
pleats and ruffs of water checked by stone flags
above the centenary flicker of a cotton-mill.
These riffles stand
over rocks that formed
from grits and sands that formed
below Carboniferous riffles.

Water was first; exulted before the Lord.

A Watering-Place

Invisible against the sky,
rain trails down the valley
past far trees.

No stile; a field-bottom wicket,
its spring formed by the bent sole of a wellington,
fixed with seven galvanised clout nails.

Quills and filaments of woodland grass
cataract over rocks and pelt downhill.
Glistening green liverworts stream for the river.

Leaves against a footbridge pier
laminate to form a skateboard ramp,
water's forever up and over
playing a five-note wobbly tea-chest obligato.

The riverbed has lit reticulations.
Each attenuated waver — confluent; overlapping —
become intenser, braver.

Ponded at flat outcrops,
or pebbling steps and shelving,
lie drifts of glowing yellow rowan leaves.

At every slab-dam and barrier,
the river stumbles over
so many winning ways.

Below a boulder ladder
light so angles at the botryoidal boiling,
its surfaces repeatedly iridesce.

In puddles, spent leaves release sweet volatiles,
fume in the memory:
under a silver-yellow shimmering skin,
the scent of slimed chrysanthemums in grave-pots
warns.

Teach me to live ...

The neighbour's photograph has caught my daughter
looking across the chain-link fence to his unseen wife.
Relaxed, arms by her sides, head up straight,
shoulders back, hair tied behind,
she wears her neat blue gingham school-dress.
Eleven, and about to start on secondary education,
the next, compulsive, breath-taking career as a woman.

Time frozen then? A moment of great promise
                                    preserved for ever?
As if a photograph could promise
any escape from the processing of negatives.

The fence's turned-down terminal hooks
march across her face and catch
at her cheek and lips.

Her clear brow? Tilts a little to the light.
Her friendly eyes? Look steadily ahead.
Her calmly smiling mouth ... she's in the process
of giving a speech of welcome:
her parted lips and tipped-up tongue
are forming the consonant 'El';
as in 'Elysium' — or just plain 'lovely'.

Convalescent

His armchair manoeuvred, awkward through doorways,
to sink into the lawn, he sits
lightly sweatered in the heat,
launching the occasional ratchetting cough:
wrenching, involuntary, welcomed as proof
that still he is too ill.
Observes the garden pondlet's surface
carpeted with mats and gas-filled boils,
comforted to know he can
do nothing now to clear it.
Idle books are idly read; at intervals;
episodes relished in the head. He's spared
the effort to share them in letters owed.
And no bells ring; no minutes pile in transit;
he isn't sent for. This pleasant lethargy:
the watching unconcerned as weeds
go wild, earth cracks, paint blisters
over rotting doors and window-frames.

But always, between dozes,
although the sun's bright haze through half-closed lids
fazes the far edge of the few days left,
the not-yet-thought-about
stealthily spreads dread fibrils:
first a fuzz, becoming hairs, then penetrating threads
which intermesh to woolly nets and mats that thicken
to the felt growth of a threat:
the full return to health.

The Eschscholtzia

Self-sown, it germinated early.
All through late autumn it struggled,
grew slowly, then stuck out the winter months.

Now, in late spring, it's taken off at last,
sucking up the opened skies, promising those summer

    flowers
whose brilliant orange scintillation
seems to proffer much more sun than they receive.

She's tidied up the bed below the shrub.
She's pulled it up.

My fault, for never talking.

Marriage Guidance: Before the First Day

I walk my twenty-month-old self
along the beach.
Forty-six years we've been tearing
at each other, little one.
Dumb, he turns on me an I
huge with rage.

The shining face you turned to me
in the wedding car
now turned away; hutched in.
I shut you out.
Will you love us whatever he makes me do?
Don't stop us having to hope.

I turn into the wind and winter sun.
The shingle flings its bitter, flinty glare.
He'll never leave us alone.
I don't know how to love myself; or you; or him.
I'm cold. I know he's bound to win.
He will — always be there.

Snap

It hangs now from a nail in his rented room.
A family holiday.
Her wary smile, seated attitude:
elbows on drawn-up knees, fore-arms lintelling legs,
right hand dangling.
"I dare not let you in" (her face
behind the door held on its chain)
and later, in large capitals in her letter:
"YOU CANNOT COME BACK HERE.
YOU CAN'T. YOU CAN'T.".

He looks at the cupboard, doorstep, jutting corner
of the wall, and wonders would he feel his head thud
thud against them, howling as he thrashed
                            from side to side
(the baby on its back, his leg chained high),
he feels the blood flood up behind each eye,
jam into cheeks and forehead, the ram applied,
breath held;
that choke on the world of the child's scream stopping:
it will not interrupt the scream to breathe
and cannot scream until it breathes again
but   not   now.   How?   When?
Neighbours.   Police.   He must go shopping.

Introduction to Suffolk

I like this land, its slow folds of soggy fields,
maintained hedgerows, copses of storm-torn oaks
partly replanted. I like, on frosty mornings, the starlings
piggy-back, warming their feet, pert partridge
clock-working their way across wheat, relaxing frights
as pheasants burst from behind banked hedges, space
to take in patterns of sugar-beet, bristling kale-stalks,
winter fields bleeding silt to the clodded roads,
deltas of sand that fan out across the tracks
from hand-deep gullies, and every day, guns
on the wooded estates.
                                    Hauling firewood on the bike
to my new, old, dank house, I re-enact the nights
of gasping grief, a mother dead, a wife
and daughter forced to make me go, a son
who can never love me, that slow,
knowing, head down, plod away
from home. I'm sorry, love. I try hard not to pine.
This soil's too gritty for plough down sillion shine.

Heart of Oak

Bark cracks and spalls, the living wood
dies, and soon softens to mealy punk
which falls away. Only the dead
dense heart remains, immune, in wind,
to moist yeasts, spreading threads, fungal decay,
but crumbed and pinhead-clotted
with an algal silver-green. Abrading slowly,
grey gouges, scoops and flutes, pleats and cusps
trail the vanished contours of those rounded
rotted girths and leaf-spread limbs.

Ouroboros IV

Around my finger runs
a ring of scaly skin.

Twenty-six years since
it was last exposed.

Red and tender,
it will heal, I s'pose:

only I will know
what metal glowed there,

what consuming worm of flame
still burns within.

Third and Fourth Generation

On top of a cupboard lie hidden
from nobody's eyes
a couple of glossy rubber magazines.
The usual boots, a few cat-suits,
a 'Mistress Dress'. Nothing too strong:
some of the girls even laughing.
Picked up at a fifth of their price;
just something to masturbate to.

At the top of their bedroom wardrobe lay hidden
a thick, matt-black, hardback book.
Turn of the century, illustrated
with frequent, rather fine engravings.
Turks used to suspend their victim
head down over a very slow fire. "However
frantically he struggled and swung, eventually
his brains would boil and burst out of his skull."

The only book my father owned.
(You're wrong; he never laid a finger on me.)

Wickedness

I was sent for the Vicar,
Reverend Wildman. I'd never been before.

When he came, in a car,
I was sent to the empty Front Room.

I could hear him, in the living room,
shouting: "I'm a wicked man".

The next day, in their bed,
that bright red, staring face.

I went for Glycerine and Lemon
"To wet his poor old lips".

I went for my son,
who hadn't cleared the table.

Was my face that startling red,
or white, with dry lips as, that night,

I left our bed and walked
away from them for ever?

Was it something that I did,
or didn't do, that struck my father down?

Am I a wicked man?
I didn't strike my son.

We are not wicked men and women:
we suffer guilt.

A Year Apart

One long goodbye we could forget
after my year away. We'd only met
at Choral Soc. that year; a year apart
would set a seal on life together.

A tour of the ship at Tilbury. The hooter blown.
In the steadily throbbing cabin:
arms unclasping, last lips, looked farewells.
But, choking at the rail, I saw you reappear
small on the already distant quay,
turn your long fair hair to one loved face
I could not see, wave bravely, turn the corner
and were gone.

A year; returned, we married, let
life's interrupted sweet duet
resume. One long goodbye beginning.
One long regret.

Lights over Sizewell

Coming out of the church
after the first night of festival readings
it's smack cold
and everyone he knows has gone.

He was head choirboy.
After his brother's wedding,
held up by the blessing in the vestry,
hanging of cassocks, ruffs and surplices,
all the notices for next day's services,
he didn't know how to enter
the back door of a pub.
At last, lost, distraught
in an empty room,
he had to be taken home and put to bed.

Walking home to the Bed and Breakfast, imagining
wine and laughter in the bright lights of the bar,
he suddenly becomes aware
that far above the orange smudge of Sizewell
fluted shafts and linen-folds of softly-glowing greens
edged or after-imaged by almost translucent reds
are slowly moving over his night.
Each second of his gaze he knows reveals
twenty times Sizewell's lifetime output
in nothing but a natural solar splendour
he never thought he'd ever see.
The Northern Lights!
They're missing the Northern Lights!

Caver

At first a certain glamour to be squirming
through water and clay,
vested in helmet, boots and boiler-suit:
to probe below the skin of sun and green,
wriggle into mysteries,
bring light to dark secrets,
follow the subterranean river down.

As they descended halls where lights
through their fume of breath petered out
at gathered swags of darkness
hanging from the vault,
descended debris from multiple collapses,
hunched under slabs fretted with former lives,
descended trenches gnawed out by water
gritting its sour teeth,
the fear of panic seeped up from primordial ruptures
and in the long knotted squeeze at the bottom
two thousand feet of consolidating faults
jammed him down:
he was blocking those behind,
failing to keep up with those ahead,
and he cried out, weeping: "I'm ill. I just can't do it"
but the guide implacably shoved at his boots,
his own wire-brushed elbows poled him through.

Alone in the central chamber
he could go no further,
must reclaim his descent.
His lamp was feeble,
but it showed him where he was
and it would last, the guide had said.

Working past, and sometimes through,
the waterfall, the limit
of that cone of light was comfort:
climbing from three feet down
to three feet up, he couldn't see
how far he had to fall.
Or still to force himself.

After scrabbling at blind ends,
lying curled inert in what
was clearly the wrong passage,
he had to admit there was no other way,
although now the deeper river
left no breathing space.
Shuddering, he plunged under.

When he emerged, breath bursting from his lips,
crawled from the swallow-hole they'd led him down
it must be, more than forty years ago,
it was still night; and no stars.
But he knew that stars would come,
the sun burst from the grey horizon.

Lunch on the Castle Lawn

Sorry; I didn't see you there.
A whole week, and I never noticed you.
Other things on my mind.

And now you're there,
I wish I'd never found you:
lips forever pursed,
always looking down on people.
Why can't you let me go?

You're just a corbel, after all;
the stone face I turned
to the ones I loved so.

A Sea Change

To lie, at last alone, in dirty sheets
I can't be bothered to wash and dry,
look at a botched and peeling ceiling,
and try whether I'm hungry enough
to get up, should not feel that strange
for I have lain on the clean white bed
of the sea and watched, so breathlessly high
above me, the glistening green glass waves
of the sky glide by.

Getting down to it

Unbox plumbing, scour with wire-wool, polish,
then lacquer each glowing roseate copper pipe,
burnished granulate pitted cast brass tap.

Take up carpets, lino, turn each filthy block
to ferric pinks, to ferrous yellow-greens;
re-herringbone this floor of local brick.

Vacuum attic cobwebs, droppings, insect husks;
take solid carborundum, plane and grind
the grubby gable wall to ruddle. Brush and seal.

Relish its longs and shorts, the brickwork set
reticulate in white lime mortar, braced and taut
to stand the shove and suck of autumn storms.

Strip off other people's patterns; rasp and scrape
leprous distemper; hack at cracked plaster;
gouge a sound brick key and only then make good.

Flake off top-coat, plough through previous finishes,
recover smothered doorframe moulding contours,
release the lines of clean-grained pine beneath old gloss.

Accept those little losses: home, job, family.
You've reached base fabric — hard-core actuality.
A sound foundation: build your own good death.

Woodburner

Last night's frost still fletches the puddle-lids:
brief sun, bright, wet-eyed; defeated.

Low-lying fields are seaside; a skating rink.
Watching a flock of rooks lift, float
and blink into light, turning to gulls.

I carry carnelian, chrysoprase, cairngorm:
armfuls of dragon-scaled, rhino-hide pine.
Sticky blue sugars clutch at my jacket.

Already a glowing dusk starches the air;
the earth will wear its stone-studded rind.
Deeper than perma-frost, I will sleep warm;
perhaps dream of pine-gums becoming amber.

Want

June sun glances silver from weathered wood,
gently, through cotton, bakes the bent back
picking strawberries. Blessing in merely passing,
it arcs the steadily cloudless.

Warm wind furls and ruffles its softest underfur
across bare arms. Exposed soil heats and tickle-pricks
for seconds the planted palm and fingers, hints at sandy
seaside days, hot towels, glinting marram,
                                        dune-slack sedge.
There's lemon and elderflower cordial in the fridge.

Tar eases between the clean new chippings where
the evening partridge hones his beak, the hare
lopes from limp sugar beet, past palings, unmown bank,
to treat himself to road-blasts of exotic tart perfume.
I sit and doze, alone. I want someone to share
this lazy intensity. I want someone to thank.

Strangers Meeting

Little one,
lying on your back,
your leg strapped high,
thrashing your head from side to side
through endless loneliness of nights
and days of pain in this strange place
of terrifying sights, fierce sounds and bitter smells,
I am not one of those
in frightening stiff white clothes
towering over your bed
who feed you, change you, wash you,
smile and try to speak kind words
but all in the wrong voices;
I am the visitor you are denied;
I feel and smell of love,
of trust and comfort;
come to me.
I will not leave you,
I wouldn't let them
carry you into the dark alone.

I whisper what you long for;
what they say, each day, trying to calm you;
but I'm not lying:
Mummy is coming to carry you home.
You weren't left here because
you are no good;
the pain, the ropes and pulleys
are no punishment.
She loves you. You are all the world to her.
You are to me.

Let your helpless rage, your anguish go.
Close your eyes and sleep now,
sleep now, little one.
Mummy is coming. Trust me:
I am you.